Tiny Spells for Big Feelings

Meditative Spells for Trauma Healing

Tiny Spells for Big Feelings

(Meditative Spells for Trauma Healing)

© 2025 by Haunted Light Productions

Disclaimer: This 'Grimoire' is a work of fiction, heavily drenched in truths and woven in magic, using creative liberties for entertainment purposes. The spells, rituals, and narratives contained within are not intended as practical guides for paranormal activity or a substitute for professional advice. Readers are encouraged to approach the content with an imaginative spirit and understand that it is for fictional enjoyment only.

All trademarks, product names, and company names mentioned herein are the property of their respective owners and are used for identification purposes only. This work is not affiliated with or endorsed by any of the brands or entities mentioned.

Some names and identifying details have been changed to protect privacy. The author's memories are shared as truthfully and faithfully as possible, filtered through lived experience and time. Any resemblance to actual persons, living or dead, or actual events is purely coincidental.

ISBN: [979-8-9995861-4-8]

First Edition: 2025

Printed in the United States of America

All Souls Welcome Here

Inside these pages live healing spells - each one pulled from the bones of my childhood, each one written in the dark and whispered toward the light. These spells were born from real moments: when I was left behind, when I stood up for myself, when I felt everything too much and all at once.

Tiny Spells for Big Feelings is a companion for anyone who has ever cried alone in their room, flinched at a slammed door, or wished they could rewrite the ending. Each spell was first cast in survival. Now, they're offered in healing.

Here, you'll find every spell from the
Spells for Surviving a Haunted Childhood series - gathered in one place, like fireflies in a jar. Plus, two never-before-told stories and the spells they taught me: one that family can cut the deepest and the other that not all secrets should stay buried.

You don't need fancy ingredients or perfect timing. You just need a feeling - and a willingness to meet it.

The truth is, spells are just one part of healing. Writing them can help you hold something heavy in a softer way, but they work best when shared alongside real support. Talk to your feelings like an old friend. Talk to a real friend. Or a therapist. Or yourself in the mirror. Let your truth echo. Let your creative freedom run wild - draw it, write it, scream it into a song if you need to. This, too, is magic.

Some of the most powerful spells I've ever cast weren't spoken - they were tasted. Or smelled. Sensory spells can ground you when words run dry. A certain scent from your childhood. A food that reminds you of a safe place. The way the air smells right before it rains. These things matter. They are portals. They are anchors. Find the smells and tastes that feel like home and use them. Often. Especially when the world feels too sharp to hold.

So open the book anywhere. Let your heart find the spell it needs the most. Whisper it out loud - *and let the magic begin*.

The Exhumed Chapters

This book holds more than just spells - it holds stories that almost slipped through the cracks. Two very dark pieces live in these pages that didn't make it into the original memoir series. Not because they weren't powerful, but because sometimes, timing is everything. These stories stayed with me. They begged inside my heart to be heard.

And now, I'm finally ready to share them - with you.

Grab a shovel, and let's dig in...

Part One
Chapter 3½
Stitched With Scrutiny

Part Three
Chapter 15½
Embarrassing Existence

PART ONE

CHAPTER
Three
1/2

Stitched With Scrutiny

This memory started with good intentions, the kind that never survives a storm in my house.

My father, for once, was home - not traveling, not drifting - and he had decided to do something kind. A gift for my grandparents. New carpet. A soft mauve meant to warm the long hallway where memories echoed too loudly and feet always moved too fast.

Nanny and Papaw picked the color themselves. My mother and father bought it. The roll was enormous, like a body waiting to be buried. Dad got to work with a box cutter and a half-lit smoke, measuring, kneeling, sweating, swearing softly to himself as he wrestled the new flooring into place.

I was his shadow. His second set of hands. I passed him tools like offerings and fetched cold cans of Dr. Pepper like a ritual. It didn't matter what the task was. What mattered was that he was there - and I was near him - the way a child clings to whatever light they can find when the sky starts to go dark.

The sound of gravel shifting warned us before the car door did. Nanny was home. The hotel she worked at must've spit her out early. The way she pulled into the drive made the house tense. Papaw met her at the door like he always did - with false comfort in a can. But it didn't matter. She came in swinging.

No hello. No, thank you. Just fury. "This is *wrong*," she snapped, not even stepping fully into the hall. "This isn't what I picked. What is *this*?"

My father stood, dust on his jeans and sweat on his brow. "This *is* what you picked," he said, already tired. "This is exactly what you told me you wanted."

But she wouldn't hear it. Wouldn't *see* it. She waved her hands like she was swatting flies, like she could banish him from her sight with enough venom. And then her words turned sharp. Cutting even.

I don't remember what she said. Just the tone. The escalation. The fire catching between them. I was still standing in the hallway when the air changed - like static before lightning. She didn't just shout.

She hurled a knife.

And in some awful twist of fate, it barely missed *me* by a whisper.

I felt the blade brush past my cheek, and then I heard my father cry out - not with fear, but with rage. Blood bloomed beneath his shirt like a curse unraveling. He yanked the knife from his own body, unbuttoned his jeans to reveal a wound just below his left hip. Flesh opened like a mouth that had been silent too long.

I found a rag. Pressed it to his side. We stumbled out the door. My hands were shaking. His words were not.

He cursed her the whole way home. A trail of fury and blood dripping behind us like breadcrumbs.

When we burst through the front door, he exploded all over again - this time at my mother.

"Do you see what *your* mother did? Do you see what she's always doing?!"

Their voices collided like cars on wet pavement. No one slowed down. Blame, denial, excuses - sirens in the walls of our living room. I don't remember how it ended. I don't think it ever really did.

But I remember the mauve carpet. It stayed. Long after stitches faded. Long after anyone talked about that day again. It sat in that hallway like a quiet ghost, holding the blood, the fight, the silence - until the house went still.

Until my grandmother took her final breath.

Spell for When
The World Cuts Too Close

Ingredients:
- A piece of paper
- A crayon, marker, or pencil
- A bandage or strip of cloth (real or pretend)
- A quiet corner to sit with your heart

Directions:
1. On the paper, draw a shape that feels like 'the hurt'. It doesn't have to make sense. Let your hand show what your words can't.

2. Place your hand on the drawing. Close your eyes. Take a breath in like you're holding something heavy. Let it out like you're finally allowed to set it down.

3. Now, pretend to wrap the shape in something soft. Use a real bandage, or your cloth, or even your own hand.

4. Hold the paper to your chest.
   Whisper:

 "This is my heart learning how to heal."

5. Fold the paper and keep it somewhere safe - a drawer, a notebook, under your pillow.

Remember:
You don't have to look at it again.
But it will remember that you were brave.

PART THREE

CHAPTER
Fifteen
1/2

Embarrassing Existence

When Dad died, I didn't know what to expect. Grief is supposed to arrive like a storm, but for me, it came wrapped in silence. I reached out to Reta - the closest thing I ever had to a mother figure, even if I never called her that. I wanted her to know, wanted someone to acknowledge the loss that felt like it swallowed the air out of my lungs.

I told her Dad had passed.

Her reply came like a cold draft through a cracked window - polite, formal, distant. A half-hearted condolence, the kind of message you send when you have to, not when you want to. There was no recognition, no warmth. No sign that I existed in that moment for her. No recognition that, in the tangled web of our family, she was the closest I'd ever had to a mother.

Weeks passed, slipping through my fingers like ashes.

I missed Dad terribly. The absence of him was a hollow ache, and I reached for anything that might fill it - a scent, a memory, a thread back to him. I remembered the cologne Dad used to wear. The one Reta bought him, a small piece of comfort I longed to hold onto. But I couldn't remember the name.

So, I reached out to Reta again.

Her response was sharper this time, clipped and dismissive. *"I have no idea what you're talking about, but best of luck on your search."*

Ten years. A decade spent with my Dad. Ten years of shared moments, memories, and life tangled together in ways I had never been allowed to understand or acknowledge. And still, she erased it all with a single sentence. Erased me with it. Made me feel like I was an embarrassment - a secret to be hidden away, something best forgotten.

Years stretched on. I was finally in therapy. Really healing for the first time. Piecing myself back together, stitch by stitch.

Then, as fate would have it, I saw her. For the first time since I was a young twenty-something. At a local store, shopping, *imagine that*. And she saw me too.

But instead of meeting my gaze, she did something I didn't expect. She ducked down like a frightened animal, hiding her face, darting for the door like a coward running from the weight of her own truth.

I laughed. Not because I was cruel, but because I was healing. Because her fear no longer held me hostage. Because I was no longer the shadow she hoped would disappear.

As I walked away, something hit me - sharp and sudden: *Why am I still keeping her secret?*

Dad is gone.

But the secret? It's hers now.

Does her family even know? Has she told anyone? Or am I still carrying a story that doesn't belong to me?

So, I wrote her daughter a letter.

I told her everything. The decade her mother spent with my Dad. How I had lived in ignorance as a child, blindsided as an adult by the truth. It was her time to know, to understand the story her mother tried to bury.

It's a shame Reta still feels the need to hide from her past. So maybe it's time to bring that past into the light.

To show it, clear as day, for all to see.

Hello, Reta. I hope you've enjoyed my books.

Spell for Unfolding
Secrets And Letting Them Go

Ingredients:
 A square of paper or cloth (something easy to fold/unfold)
 Your hands and your breath
 A quiet place where you can move slowly and listen

Directions:
1. **Hold the square flat in your hands.** Imagine your secret is folded inside it - quiet, waiting.

2. The secret grows tight inside the folds. Breathe deeply and say: *"It does not own me."*

3. **Now unfold the square completely.** Let it stretch open, wide and free. Imagine your secret loosening, no longer trapped. Whisper: *"I release what was hidden. I choose to be seen."*

4. **Hold the open square out in front of you.** Feel the space around it - light, air, possibility. Say aloud: *"My truth unfolds with strength and grace."*

Remember:
 Place the unfolded square somewhere light can reach it - a windowsill, your altar, or a place you visit often. Let your secret live in the open air - no longer tucked and folded away.

 "Secrets held in shadow lose their power in the light."

Your Feelings Matter

Some spells are too small to speak aloud.
One's whispered through clenched teeth or bitten
tongues, Tucked inside tear-streaked cheeks and
nightlight-lit wishes.

You may not have known you were casting them.
When you buried a scream in your pillow,
When you stood still so no one would notice you crying,
When your chest ached, but no one asked -

Those were all spells, too.

The big feelings - they came like storms.

But *you*?

You built a shelter with your choices,
stitched skies with your breath,
Hid thunder beneath your ribs.

This book isn't here to fix you.
It's here to honor the version of you that survived -
Without ever being taught how.

Each page is a charm.

Each truth, a talisman.

Each feeling, a flare of power too bright to stay buried.

Spells for Surviving a Haunted Childhood
(Part One)

ONE | Spell for Braving the Cold

TWO | Spell for When the Gaze Feels Too Heavy

THREE | Spell for What You Can't Say Out Loud

FOUR | Spell for Illuminating the Shadows

FIVE | Spell for When the Light Leaves the Room Too Soon

SIX | Spell for When You Aren't Believed

SEVEN | Spell for the Things That Disappear Too Quickly

EIGHT | Spell for When the Ground Begins to Shake

NINE | Spell for When Time Stands Too Still

TEN | Spell for the Forgotten Child

ELEVEN | Spell for Magic No One Else Can See

TWELVE | Spell for When the Grip Is Too Tight

THIRTEEN | Spell for Disappearing Without Leaving

FOURTEEN | Spell for When No One Is Coming to Save You

FIFTEEN | Spell for When the Air Gets Too Thick to Breathe

SIXTEEN | Spell for When They Leave Without Looking Back

SEVENTEEN | Spell for When You Feel Like No One Cares

EIGHTEEN | Spell for Walking the Line Between Fantasy and Truth

NINETEEN | Spell for Taking a Leap of Faith

TWENTY | Spell for When You Want to Believe

Spell for
Braving the Cold

Ingredients:

One red mitten (even if lost)
Three deep breaths of winter air
A golden thread - for warmth
The memory of a safe voice calling your name

Directions:

1. Close your eyes and breathe in deeply. Imagine the wind rushing in your ears.

2. Remember the feeling of being small, but not alone.

3. Say this:

> "I remember the snow and the silence,
> and how it tried to take me.
> But I was not swallowed. I was seen.
> I was found.
> I carry warmth in my bones,
> passed down from hands that held me.
> The cold does not get to have me. I belong to the light."

Repeat until the snow stops falling inside your heart.

Spell for When
The Gaze Feels Too Heavy

Ingredients:

One blanket pulled tightly over your head
Three soft breaths to calm a racing heart
The sound of your own name, spoken kindly
A memory of someone who saw you without scorn

Directions:

1. Close your eyes and make your body small - not in fear, but in protection.

2. Picture a mirror that only shows the good parts.

3. Whisper:

> "I am not a thing to be stared at.
> I am not a doll or a burden or a mistake.
> I am a child of light, even in rooms full of shadow.
> You may watch me, but you will not break me."

Repeat until the air feels safe again.

Spell for
What You Can't Say Out Loud

Ingredients:

One Barbie, half-dressed
One hairbrush used on half-brushed hair
A silence you mistook for safety
A voice swallowed in your own throat

Directions:

1. Sit quietly and hold what remains.

2. Picture the way her voice used to sound.

3. Say this:

> "I see the effort between the silences.
> I remember when it almost felt like enough.
> Even broken love has a shape - and I can
> carry its outline without letting it shape me.
> I do not disappear. I become."

Repeat until your own voice comes back.

Spell for
Illuminating the Shadows

Ingredients:

The creak of a porch rocking chair
The echo of a theme song in the kitchen
The hum of summer cicadas
A man who always showed up

Directions:

1. Sit in a patch of sunlight, even if it's small.

2. Close your eyes and breathe in the memory of someone who made you feel safe.

3. Say this:

> "I remember the light in the dark.
> I remember hands that steadied without squeezing.
> I carry safety in my cells now, passed down through steadiness.
> The storm may return - but I will always find the porch."

Repeat when the world feels too loud to stay in your body.

Spell for When
The Light Leaves the Room Too Soon

Ingredients:

A candle burnt out with much more life to give
One folded blanket, heavy with memory
The final word you never got to say
A sliver of childhood, quietly cracked

Directions:

1. Sit in the quietest part of your home.

2. Wrap the blanket around your shoulders - even if it no longer holds warmth

3. Hold the unlit candle in your hands.

4. Whisper the name of the one you lost, three times.

5. Let the silence answer.

> "I carry you in the hush between heartbeats.
> I name the absence so it doesn't swallow me whole.
> I let the darkness sit beside me -
> but I do not hand it the reins."

Repeat whenever the darkness becomes blinding.

Spell for
When You Aren't Believed

Ingredients:

One missing piece
A truth no one heard
A closed door
An empty folded tissue (tear soaked is fine)

Directions:

1. Hold the truth in your palm like a stone.

2. Whisper it into the dark three times.

3. Breathe in silence. Breathe out shame.

> "I know what I saw. I know what I held. Even if no one else believes me - I do."

Repeat until your voice returns.

Spell for The Things
That Disappear Too Quickly

Ingredients:

One memory you almost forgot
A drawer left empty
A scent that makes your chest ache
Silence thick as syrup

Directions:

1. Write down what you remember before it fades.

2. Hold it in your palm like it's still warm.

3. Whisper their name into the quiet.

> "I keep you in the spaces no one thinks to look.
> Between the heartbeats,
> Behind the words,
> Beneath the sadness.
> You are not lost.
> You are just hidden - from her."

Spell for When the
Ground Begins to Shake

Ingredients:

One empty lunchbox, closed but echoing
A tear that never fell
A joke you didn't find funny
The sound of a steering wheel gripped too tightly

Directions:

1. Find a quiet place where no one is watching.
Sit with your back against the wall - the way you used to when the
house felt unstable.

2. Open the lunchbox and whisper inside it:

> "I was small, but I noticed everything."

3. Hold your breath for five seconds. Then exhale, and with it, let go
of the lie that your feelings made things worse.

4. Tap your heart once with your palm. Say:

> "This quake is not my fault.
> This silence is not my shape.
> I *am* allowed to feel."

5. Close the lunchbox. Let the echo greet you next time you open
an empty lunchbox.

*Repeat when you feel yourself shrinking to fit a world too brittle
to hold you.*

Spell for
When Time Stands Too Still

Ingredients:

One crayon - clutched too tightly
A slammed door still ringing in your ears
A porch light that never flickered back on
A clock stuck on midnight

Directions:

1. Sit in the quiet after the storm - not to silence it, but to hear what's left behind.

2. Hold the crayon in your palm. Let it remind you: even small things can leave marks.

3. Close your eyes and picture the ticking clock. Say the words:

> "Even when the hands won't move,
> Even when no one opens the door,
> Even when love leaves the room - I remain."

4. Breathe. In through what was lost. Out through what you're becoming.

Repeat when you need to remember that you didn't vanish with them.

Spell for
The Forgotten Child

Ingredients:

One name no one ever says aloud
A photo face down in a drawer
Three sighs that never found their voice
A patch of moonlight that no one claims
silence, aged and sharpened

Directions:

1. Begin at dusk. Not because it's magic - but because that's when the ache returns.

2. Find a quiet corner where no one has ever looked for you. Sit there until the air begins to hum.

3. Take the name you were given, the one they stopped using, and whisper it to the walls. Let the sound remind you.

4. Press your palms to the floor. Tell the Earth your story - not for justice, not for revenge - but so someone knows. Even if it's just the floorboards.

> *"I was never the problem. I was the spell they were too afraid to cast."*

Spell for Magic
No One Else Can See

Ingredients:

One object everyone else calls worthless
A memory that won't let go
A hush that lives between blinks
One breath held too long

Directions:

1. Sit with your back to the wall and your heart facing forward.

2. Hold the object, even if only in your mind.

3. Whisper to it: "I see you. I remember."

4. Let the magic rise, even if no one else believes it's there.

> "Some things don't need to be fixed to matter. Some things are powerful just by surviving."

Repeat until the quiet feels sacred, not empty.

Spell for
When the Grip Is Too Tight

Ingredients:

A torn piece of fabric
A place you can be alone (closets count)
A candle imagined in your mind
One truth you're brave enough to whisper

Directions:

1. Sit in your chosen space. Let the quiet settle first. Let it crawl into your lap like an old friend.

2. Close your eyes and light the candle in your mind. Watch the flame dance. Watch how it never flinches.

3. Whisper this spell, even if your voice shakes:

> "This hurt is not mine to keep.
> These hands did not make me.
> This fear is not my forever.
> I am not the broken thing they tried to make."

4. Picture a door opening in your chest. Let the pain walk through it. Let the darkness follow, not to haunt you, but to carry what you cannot.

5. Blow out the candle (even if it was only pretend). Let the silence say: you survived.

"If they ever tell you it didn't happen, show them your silence.

Show them how even shadows remember."

Spell for
Disappearing Without Leaving

Ingredients:

One can of cold soup
A sock without its pair
A radio playing low enough to whisper
Dust from under the couch
A hallway shadow that knows your name

Directions:

1. Sit in the doorway of your room. Right where the carpet thins from pacing.

2. Line up the ingredients in front of you. Don't speak. Just notice them. They're proof you existed today.

3. Whisper your own name like a question. Whisper it again like a fact.

4. Place your hand over your chest. If you feel anything at all - that's enough. That's the proof.

> "Even if they don't see me,
> Even if they never did -
> I am here. I am still here."

Repeat whenever silence becomes too loud.

Spell for
When No One Is Coming to Save You

Ingredients:

A blanket pulled over your shoulders like a knight's cape
The glow of a flashlight under the covers
Three deep breaths taken while no one is looking
Your truest wish, a tiny whisper only the dust bunnies can hear

Directions:

1. Find a quiet corner - a closet works best, especially one that smells like old wood and kept secrets.

2. Turn off every light except the one you made yourself - a flashlight, a TV screen left glowing, a night light shaped like a star.

3. Whisper to your stuffed animals. Line them up like witnesses. Give them names. Let them cheer for you.

4. Close your eyes and build your own circus - from dust, from shadows, from all the glittering things they said you were too small to understand. Imagine lions roaring just for you. Imagine music that never lies. Imagine someone clapping just because you're brave.

7. Now take three deep breaths. Inhale like you're breathing in magic. Exhale like you're letting go of every lie they told you about being unworthy of love.

8. Hold your breath for one heartbeat more - just long enough to feel the silence. Just long enough to know *you're still here.*

Spell for When
The Air Gets Too Thick to Breathe

Ingredients:

One mirror fogged over with silence
The outline of your body in the dark
A breath you forgot you were holding
The memory of your name, hidden in a corner

Directions:

1. Sit somewhere dim, somewhere quiet. Let the room blur at the edges.

2. Close your eyes. Inhale slowly, as if the air weighs more now. Exhale like you're trying not to wake the house.

3. Picture the fog. Let it come. Let it wrap you up. Let it see you.

4. When your chest starts to tighten, place your hand flat against your heart. Feel the proof.

5. Whisper, even if only in your mind:

> "I am still here.
> Even when the room forgets me.
> Even when my voice won't come.
> Even when I disappear to survive—
> I am still here."

Repeat any time the air gets too heavy.

Spell for When They Leave Without Looking Back

Ingredients:

One ribbon dropped on the road
A stuffed dog - hugged too tightly
The echo of a slammed door
The silence after footsteps fade

Directions:

1. Sit by the window where you last saw them. Let the light (or the darkness) fall on your face.

2. Wrap the ribbon around your wrist. Not to remember them - to remember *you*.

3. Hold the stuffed dog in both hands. It's heavy with memory. It will not break. Neither will you.

4. Whisper to the air, to the ghosts, to yourself:

> "You left.
> But I stayed.
> And still, I rise."

Repeat as needed - especially when it feels like their leaving was your fault. But just remember, it never was.

Spell for When You Feel Like No One Cares

Ingredients:

A single candle no one bothered to light
The silence after a missed birthday
One strand of mist (imagined or remembered)
A drop of rain saved in memory's palm
Your name, spoken only in your own voice

Directions:

1. Find a quiet space. A porch. A stairwell. A bedroom corner. Somewhere that knows your stillness.

2. Sit with your knees to your chest and press one hand against your heartbeat. Not to stop it—just to prove it's still there.

3. Close your eyes. Let the forgotten moments rise. Let them speak.

4. Whisper this, aloud or inside:

> "Even if no one lit the candle,
> I am still a flame.
> Even if no one called my name,
> I shall remain.
> The rain remembers.
> The mist mourns.
> And I—
> I will forever endure."

You are enough. You always have been, and you always will be.

Spell for Walking The Line
Between Fantasy and Truth

Ingredients:

One soggy postcard
A lion with no roar
A piece of frayed rope
A child's question left unanswered

Directions:

1. Stand at the center of your disappointment. Let it tower over you. Let it rot.

2. Breathe in the mildew from the scent of the postcard and make it your proof.

3. Tie the frayed rope around your wrist-not to hold you back, but to remind you.

4. Say aloud:

"I saw it all. And I still chose better."

Repeat whenever the fantasy calls you back.
Remember: you are not the one who disappeared.

Spell for
Taking a Leap of Faith

Ingredients:

One folded paper crown
A shoelace knotted with hope
The first French fry shared across a booth
A mile marker that feels like a new beginning

Directions:

1. Buckle your heart. Roll down the window.

2. Let the past fall behind you like dust.

3. When you see the road curve north, whisper:

> "Not all knights wear armor. Some drive
> old trucks and call you baby girl."

Repeat as needed. Especially when doubt starts to whisper again.

Spell for
When You Want to Believe

Ingredients:

One porch light, left on for you
Three brave wishes whispered into a pillow
The tiniest room where hope can grow
A shape you almost don't see

Directions:

1. Step into the space made for you.

2. Name it "home," even if your voice shakes.

3. Let the light touch your skin and say, "I am safe here."

4. When the shadows return, do not greet them. Let them pass like the weather.

> "Some spells don't chase the dark away.
> They teach you how to bloom *without* light."

Repeat any time you're feeling lost and alone.

SPELLS FOR SURVIVING A HAUNTED CHILDHOOD
(PART TWO)

ONE | Spell for How to Make a Best Friend

TWO | Spell for Finding Your Strength

THREE | Spell for Making Any Place a Home

FOUR | Spell for How to Activate Your Super Strength

FIVE | Spell for When You Feel Like You Will Never Measure Up

SIX | Spell for When the Floodgates Open

SEVEN | Spell for When You're Not the One Hurting This Time

EIGHT | Spell for When the Darkness Under Your Bed Grows Teeth

NINE | Spell for When You Feel Left Out

TEN | Spell for When Something You Loved Becomes a Memory

ELEVEN | Spell for When Things Are Out of Your Control

TWELVE | Spell for When You Mistake the Fire for Warmth

THIRTEEN | Spell for When You're Ready to Let Go

FOURTEEN | Spell for When the Loneliness Overwhelms You

FIFTEEN | Spell for When You Just Want to Leave

SIXTEEN | Spell for When the Truth Sheds Its Skin

SEVENTEEN | Spell for When You Feel Like a Ghost at Your Own Celebration

EIGHTEEN | Spell for When You're Ready to Begin Again

NINETEEN | Spell for When You Need To Speak the Unspeakable

TWENTY | Spell for When You Make it Out Alive - Just Barely

Spell for
How to Make a Best Friend

Ingredients:

One genuine compliment

The courage to speak first

A shared snack (optional but helpful)

A quiet kind of knowing

Directions:

1. Look around. There's someone else watching the world like you do - softly, carefully. Find them.

2. Say something kind. Even if your voice trembles.

3. Listen for the echo. The kind reply. The soul that recognizes yours.

4. When the moment feels right, sit beside them. Share something small.

> "Real friendship does not require performance. Only presence."

5. Return again. And again. Until returning feels like home.

Spell for
Finding Your Strength

Ingredients:

One deep breath held in your chest like a secret
The memory of a time you stood up
(for yourself or someone else)
A mirror that doesn't lie, even when you wish it would
A whisper said only to yourself: "Not this time."

Directions:

1. Close your eyes.

2. Picture the version of you that used to shrink. The one who made herself small to survive.

3. Thank her. She kept you safe.

4. Say this out loud three times

> "I don't shrink anymore.
> Now I rise."

Repeat when your arms feel like jelly and your legs too shaky to stand.

Spell for Making
Any Place a Home

Ingredients:

One key placed with care in a small palm
Three deep breaths taken before you cross the threshold
Something to call your own (a pillow, a mug, a corner of sunlight)
A memory you want to grow roots from

Directions:

1. Enter slowly. Let your footsteps greet the floor like an old friend.

2. Find a corner that calls your name - even if it's cracked or dusty.

3. Place your chosen object there. Say aloud, "This is mine."

4. Whisper something kind into the walls. Even if they don't believe you yet, they will.

5. Each day, add something: a drawing, a song, a meal, a breath.

6. When the shadows return (they always do), turn on the light and remind them: "You may linger, but you do not lead."

"Home is not built with walls. It's built with presence. Even if yours is the only one that stays."

Spell for How To
Activate Your Super Strength

Ingredients:

One deep breath, the kind that fills every inch of your lungs
The voice that says "No", even when your throat wants to close
The memory of your feet hitting pavement as you run as fast as you can
Shadows that stand beside you, not behind you
And a kick fueled by every time someone made you feel small

Directions:

1. The moment fear grips your spine, pause.

2. Feel your hands, your stance, your breath.

3. Let the shadow guide you - not into darkness, but through it.

4. You are not what happened to you. Know your power and never forget it.

> "I will not be small.
> I will not be silent.
> I have survived before.
> I will do it again."

Repeat every time you need backup.

Spell for When You Feel
Like You Will Never Measure Up

Ingredients:
One ruler (wooden, worn, or plastic - anything that's tried to define you)
A mirror you can sit with
A safe, quiet place where no one's watching
Seven truths about yourself you've hidden from sight to survive

Directions:
1. Sit with the ruler stretched before you, like a line someone else once dared you to walk.

2. Face the mirror. See yourself - not as a reflection, but as a witness.

3. For each inch on the ruler, speak one truth. Begin with the smallest. Let your voice grow.

Inch by Inch:

Inch 1 - *I am not what they said I was.*
Inch 2 - *I am not a reflection of their shame.*
Inch 3 - *I am growing, even if they don't see it.*
Inch 4 - *Their rules were not made for me.*
Inch 5 - *I hold more than they ever measured.*
Inch 6 - *I will not shrink to fit their frame.*
Inch 7 - *I am already enough.*

Place the ruler under your pillow, your notebook, or your heart.

> "It no longer measures your worth.
> It only marks the places you began to rise."

Repeat as needed. Especially when their voices start sounding like your own.

Spell for When
the Floodgates Open

Ingredients:

One framed photo of a time you miss
A glass of water, filled to the brim
A pillow that remembers your shape

Directions:

1. Sit in the quiet. Let the stillness fill the room.

2. Place the glass of water beside the photo. This is the before.

3. Cry. Let it come. Don't chase it back into your chest. Don't apologize for the sound.

4. When you're ready, press the photo to your chest and whisper:

> "This storm has a name,
> And it is mine to weather."

5. Pour the glass of water out the window or into the earth. This is the after.

6. Lie down. Let your pillow hold the weight. Let the darkness sit with you, not above you.

> *"Some rain must fall before the sun remembers where you live.*
> *Let it come. Let it pass. You are still here."*

Spell for When You're
Not the One Hurting This Time

Ingredients:

A flickering television

One friend who understands too much, too young

Popcorn, never burnt

A room with the door closed

The sound of something breaking in the other room

Directions:

1. Sit shoulder to shoulder.

2. Don't ask questions you already know the answers to.

3. Turn the TV up until it drowns out the storm.

4. When the Darkness enters, don't flinch. Just offer it a seat.

5. Hold your breath. Hold your friend's hand. Hold your own heart steady.

> "This time the pain isn't mine.
> But I still feel it.
> I still see it.
> I will sit here and bear witness.
> I will not run.
> I will not speak.
> I will survive.
> We both will."

Spell for When the Darkness Under Your Bed Grows Teeth

Ingredients:

A meal you didn't finish
A door that shut too quietly
A truth no one wants to say out loud
A pair of tired eyes that used to look at you like you mattered
One monster, known by name

Directions:

1. Lie still in the quiet.

2. Feel the weight of the words that were never said.

3. Let the tears come - silent, slow, honest.

4. Reach beneath your bed.

5. Do not flinch when you feel it watching.

6. Whisper your secret into the dark.

> "I know you're there.
> I know what you've seen.
> I know what I've lost.
> So stay.
> Guard me.
> Witness me.
> I will play the part they cast me in,
>
> But you will know who I really am."

Spell for
When You Feel Left Out

Ingredients:

One unopened packet of ketchup
A $20 bill that smells like arcade grease
Two fake smiles balanced like scales
One real laugh (yours, or someone who sees you)
A friendship that wraps around your ribs like armor

Directions:

1. Sit in the backseat. Watch the lines on the highway blur into memory.

2. Let the silence fill up your lungs. Let it sting.

3. Pull the spell from your pocket - the one shaped like a friend's hand.

4. Whisper the words no one else hears:

> "I may not be what they came for,
> But I am *still* here.
> I take up space.
> I breathe.
> I belong, even if they forget to make room.
> My worth does not need their permission."

Then do the boldest thing of all:

Laugh anyway.
Hold your joy tight.
Let them be confused by your shine.

Spell for When Something You Loved Becomes a Memory

Ingredients:

One basketball with your name written in faded ink
A crumpled pay stub
The last spoonful of chocolate ice cream from the bowl
A parking lot that stays full long after everyone has left
One breath of freedom pressed into the palm of your hand

Directions:

1. Lay the object down gently.
  You know the one - the thing you thought would be forever.

2. Don't speak. Just listen to the silence it leaves behind.

3. Stir your ice cream until it melts into memory.

4. Turn the key in your own ignition. Feel the engine wake up.

5. Whisper:

> "I am not who I was.
> I am not who they forgot.
> I am the driver now.
> I am the rhythm.
> I don't need a court to keep score."

Repeat when you are forced to choose between what
you need and what you want.

Spell for When Things
Are Out of Your Control

Ingredients:

A bottle half-full of something sweet

The sound of a siren from far away

One name whispered into a pillow

A clock that forgot to tick

Directions:

1. Stand at the threshold of any room you love.

2. Hold the bottle in both hands and listen - really listen - to the silence.

3. Whisper their name once. Then say:

> "I can't fix it. I can't stop it.
> But I can feel it.
> And I won't look away."

Repeat only when the sky feels too big and the ground too far away.

Spell for When You Mistake the Fire for Warmth

Ingredients:

A lie you told to keep someone close
A cardigan too heavy to take off
The shadow of someone who should've noticed

Directions:

1. Sit in the place you return to, even when it hurts.

2. Breathe. Deeply. In with hope. Out with past regrets.

3. Whisper:

> "I thought I was safe.
> I thought I was seen.
> But now I know -
> Some fires *only* burn."

Repeat this spell when old flames call you home.

Spell for
When You're Ready to Let Go

Ingredients:

A day you almost didn't survive

A name you miss but cannot call

A pill bottle you no longer open

The silence that swallowed your scream

Directions:

1. Sit with the shadow of who you used to be.

2. Close your eyes and place your hand on your heart.

3. Whisper:

> *"I thought the end was the only exit.*
> *But maybe - just maybe -*
> *There's a door I haven't tried yet."*

4. Stand up.

5. Walk toward it. Even if your legs shake.

You don't need to know where it leads. You just need to believe it's not too late.

Spell for When
The Loneliness Overwhelms You

Ingredients:

One breath you didn't think you could take
The sound of your own heartbeat in an empty room
A name you stopped saying out loud
A blanket that smells like the last place you felt safe
The Darkness (only if it volunteers)

Directions:

1. Sit where the silence is thickest.

2. Place your hand on your chest. Feel it. That's proof. You're still here.

3. Whisper your name once, then again. As if someone else needs to know it.

4. Let the tears come. Don't fight them. They are the water in which your strength learns to swim.

5. Close your eyes and imagine arms around you - not his, not hers, but yours. Strong. Unmoving. Forgiving.

> *"I am not empty.*
> *I am not forgotten.*
> *I am not the things they did to me."*

7. Let the darkness curl beside you, not to haunt - but to guard.

Sleep, if you can. Breathe, if you must. But promise yourself: this is not the end of your story.

Spell for
When You Just Want to Leave

Ingredients:

One packed bag, zipped up too fast
A body that keeps moving, even when the soul won't
A road you don't remember choosing
A name you stopped answering to

Directions:

1. Sit in the passenger seat of your life. Watch the trees blur. Let the silence hum.

2. Do not apologize for needing to go - even if you don't know where you're going.

3. Take out your phone. Delete the messages you hoped would come.

4. Whisper your old name into the window fog and trace a new one beside it.

5. When the ache rises, don't swallow it - write it down. Burn the page.

> "I am not what I left behind.
> I am not who they remember.
> I am the person I'm trying to become."

Repeat until you stop checking the rearview mirror.

Spell for When the Truth Sheds Its Skin

Ingredients:

One gut feeling you were told to ignore
A secret pulled into the light
The sound of laughter in the wrong place
One clean getaway

Directions:

1. Sit with the truth until it stops shaking.

2. Let it wrap around your shoulders like armor, not shame.

3. Look each version of the story in the eye - then choose your own.

4. Walk forward. Even if your legs tremble.

> "Some truths crawl. Some truths sting.
> But this one shed its skin - and freed
> me."

Repeat if you ever forget how to trust your instincts.

Spell for When You Feel Like a Ghost at Your Own Celebration

Ingredients:

A letter you wrote for your eyes only
A smile they can't understand
A fire they tried to dim
One quiet, undeniable truth

Directions:

1. Hold a candle in the quiet - no witnesses.

2. Whisper your full name with love in your voice.

3. Close your eyes and see the moment:

4. Envision the crowd cheering. Just for you. Feel the fire in your chest.

5. Say it loud, even if only to yourself:

> *'They don't get to rewrite my story. I'm the one holding the pen.'*

Repeat as needed, especially when they come with cameras and clean consciences.

Spell for When You're Ready to Begin Again

Ingredients:

One key that rattles with potential
A window that lets the light back in
A soft place to land (even if it's just a
hand-me-down couch)
A voice that says, "I'm allowed to want more."

Directions:

1. Sweep the floor of old doubts.

2. Open every drawer like it's a doorway to something better.

3. Place one hope in every corner.

4. Sit cross-legged in the center and say:

> "I may not know where I'm going.
> But I know where I won't stay."

5. Then turn on the lights. *This is your home now.*

Spell for When You
Need To Speak the Unspeakable

Ingredients:

One fire buried inside you for far too long
A name no one wanted you to say
A truth older than silence
The exit wound of betrayal

Directions:

1. Stand up taller than the memory of being small.

2. Say it. Even if your voice shakes. Especially if it does.

3. Don't apologize for the sound it makes.

4. Leave the door open only wide enough for your shadow.

> "I am not your secret.
>   I am not your shame.
>   I am not your scapegoat.
>   I am the thunder you tried to silence."

Speak it until the house shakes. Then walk out with your newfound power.

Spell For When You
Make It Out Alive - Just Barely

Ingredients:

One scar that doesn't hurt anymore

A map folded too many times

A name you reclaimed

One ounce of belief - hard-earned and holy

Directions:

1. Light a candle with your own fire. The kind from inside your own heart.

2. Place your palm over your chest. Feel your heartbeat. Breathe.

3. Speak aloud:

> "I was built to break,
> But I didn't.
> Instead, I choose to rise.
> This is not the end.
> This is the moment I begin."

Repeat until you feel the warmth of your own fire again.

Spells for Surviving a Haunted Childhood
(Part Three)

ONE | Spell for Clearing the Room With Only Your Voice

TWO | Spell to Find the Courage to Introduce Yourself

THREE | Spell for How to Mend Broken Fences

FOUR | Spell for When It's Time to Shatter the Illusion

FIVE | Spell for When Something Finds Its Way Back to You

SIX | Spell for When the Question Is Bigger Than the Answer

SEVEN | Spell for When You're Afraid Joy Isn't Yours to Keep

EIGHT | Spell for When You Finally Feel Loved

NINE | Spell for Choosing You, Always

TEN | Spell for Recognizing a Message from the Universe

ELEVEN | Spell for Becoming the Parent You Never Had

TWELVE | Spell for Holding On When It All Falls Apart (Again)

THIRTEEN | Spell to Freeze Time (For Just a Little While)

FOURTEEN | Spell for Saying Goodnight Forever

FIFTEEN | Spell for When the Ocean of Grief Tries to Swallow You

SIXTEEN | Spell for the Kind of Love That Waits

SEVENTEEN | Spell for the Grace of Forgiveness

EIGHTEEN | Spell for When Time Moves Too Fast

NINETEEN | Spell for Returning to Your True Self

TWENTY | Spell for When You're Ready to Hear the Little Voice Inside You

Spell for Clearing The Room With Only Your Voice

Ingredients:

A house full of ghosts

One truth that no longer fits

A voice you almost forgot you had

Directions:

1. Sweep the room with your presence. Not anger. Not fear. Just presence.

2. Speak once, like you mean it.

3. Let the silence that follows be your protection spell.

> "This is mine.
> You don't get to stay here anymore.
> I decide who stays
> And who goes."

Repeat as needed until the house knows your name again.

Spell to Find The Courage to Introduce Yourself

Ingredients:

One tremble of uncertainty
A deep breath from the bottom of your ribs
A sentence with your own name in it
A little bit of hope

Directions:

1. Walk toward what feels unfamiliar but safe.

2. Speak your name aloud.

3. Let your voice shake if it needs to.

4. Sit. Stay. Listen.

5. Watch for the light.

> *"Not all open doors creak.*
> *Some wait quietly for you to knock."*

Repeat when you're ready to open yourself up to someone new.

Spell for How to
Mend Broken Fences

Ingredients:

A plank of patience
Three nails of grace
A hammer of honesty
One honest look backward
One hopeful look forward

Directions:

1. Survey the damage. Don't flinch. Don't pretend it wasn't there.

2. Gather your tools. You'll need more forgiveness than you thought.

3. Start with one post - one honest conversation, one quiet offering of trust.

4. When it wobbles, brace it. When it cracks again, try another angle.

5. Paint over the splinters if you want, just don't forget they're there.

> "Not every fence needs to be perfect.
> Just strong enough to stand through the next storm."

Repeat when ready to let someone in again.

Spell for When
It's Time to Shatter the Illusion

Ingredients:

One mirror, hand-held or heart-sized
A truth you've been avoiding
Three deep breaths you forgot you were holding
A surface strong enough to catch what breaks

Directions:

1. Hold the mirror in both hands and let it see you - all of you, even the parts that flinch.

2. Speak the truth aloud. No softness. Just the truth, raw and whole.

3. Press your reflection gently with your thumb. Ask: "Was any of this ever real?"

4. If the answer echoes, it's time. Shatter inside your mind, carefully. (A whisper will do, even if the glass stays intact.)

> "What I saw was never the truth.
> What I believed was never the whole story.
> Let the illusion fall like glass -
> Not to hurt me,
> But to free me."

Repeat when you're ready to finally hold what's real.

Spell for When Something Finds Its Way Back to You

Ingredients:

One object you thought you'd lost
A heart open enough to receive it
Two hands steady enough to hold it again
One moment that feels too big for logic

Directions:

1. Gently turn the object in your hand, once clockwise. Then once counterclockwise.

2. Whisper your name into its fabric, like a reminder: *I'm still here.*

3. Don't ask *why.* Ask *what now?*

> "Some things return not because they were lost,
>   but because you are ready to remember."

Repeat as needed. Especially when the universe whispers instead of shouts.

Spell for When the Question Is Bigger Than the Answer

Ingredients:

A quiet kitchen
Someone who sees your future
A storm you've almost survived
One deep breath

Directions:

1. Sit with the question - don't rush it.

2. Let your heartbeat speak louder than fear.

3. Say yes to the moment, even if you're unsure about forever.

>"Some answers don't come in words.
>They come in time.
> In trust.
> In faith.
>And a little bit of *magic*."

Repeat when you just need a minute to *breathe* and *think*.

Spell for When You're Afraid Joy Isn't Yours to Keep

Ingredients:

One quiet moment that feels too good to be true
A memory that still aches in your chest
An item that reminds you of what's real
Two hands willing to stay open, even if they tremble

Directions:

1. Sit somewhere soft, where your shoulders can unclench.

2. Hold the object in both hands - like you're holding joy itself.

3. Let the doubt rise. Let it speak. Then answer it. Whisper:

>	"I am allowed to have this."

4. If the Darkness appears, don't flinch. Look it in the face - even if only in your mind - and say:

>	"Not this time."

Repeat as needed. Especially when hope feels too quiet to trust.

Spell for When
You Finally Feel Loved

Ingredients:

A question asked under trembled breath

A patch of sand with your name written

A piece of jewelry that makes you feel strong

A quiet place beneath stars - real or remembered

Directions:

1. Write your name in the sand where the tide can't reach.

2. Speak your desires aloud, even if your voice trembles.

3. When the fireworks come, don't look away

4. Put on the jewelry. Let it catch the light. Let it remind you who you are and where you're going.

5. Say these words:

> 'The night sky shines like a road map to peace, and I am ready for what's next.'

Repeat when the signs seem too good to be true.

Spell for Choosing You, Always

To be spoken together, or offered as a quiet vow. No outside ingredients needed - just breath, presence, and a willingness to stay.

Say this together:
I will choose you -

> *In every season,*
> *In every storm,*
> *In every version of tomorrow.*

I choose you - not just for the light,
But for the days that don't go right.

When the light is golden,
I will stand beside you in gratitude.
When the clouds are gray,
I will stay beside you in grace.

When we are laughing,
I will hold your hand.
When we are hurting,
Forever, I'll be your best friend.

To have and to hold,
for you -
My love will never fold.

I choose you - for now and for always.
I will love you for all of my days.

Spell for Recognizing
A Message from the Universe

Ingredients:

One object from your past, returned to you by chance

A quiet place where signs can be heard

A deep breath, in and out

Trust

Directions:

1. Hold the object. Don't overthink it. Just feel.

2. Close your eyes, and picture all the places it's been. All the time it's traveled. All the ways it found its way back.

3. Say aloud:

> "I see it. I see the sign.
> I am not forgotten.
> I am on the path."

4. Thank the moment. Even if you don't understand it all yet. You will.

5. Move forward. Carry it with you, not as baggage, but as belief.

Repeat when you need to believe in something bigger than yourself.

Spell for Becoming
The Parent You Never Had

Ingredients:

One lullaby sung through tears
A baby blanket that smells like milk and sleep
The memory of a mother's absence
The presence of a child's need

Directions:

1. Whisper their name in the quiet before dawn.

2. Let her tiny fingers wrap around yours.

3. Rock her, even if no one ever rocked you.

4. Let the tears fall - they're part of the spell.

5. Say: "I will be what I never had. I will give what I never got. And that will be enough."

Repeat when the emotions get too heavy to hold.

Spell For Holding On
When It All Falls Apart (Again)

Ingredients:

One text message you didn't think anyone would read

A locked door, a quiet cry

Two hands reaching through the noise

A bridge held together by truth

Directions:

1. Whisper your fears to someone who loves you.

2. Let them hear *all* of it.

3. If they stay, build a bridge with them.

4. If they leave, light a candle, even if only in your mind, and stay anyway.

Remember:

This time, you are the one who holds.

Spell to Freeze Time
(For Just a Little While)

Ingredients:

One camera (film, digital, or imaginary - anything to help you see)
Golden light (sunset preferred, but bedside lamp will do)
One moment you never want to forget
Steady hands and a tender heart

Directions:

1. Find the light. It doesn't have to be perfect - just real. The way it catches your baby's hair.

2. Lift your camera (or your gaze). Look through the lens - not just at what's there, but at what you want to remember.

3. Steady your breath. Hold it if you must - *this is where the magic lives.*

4. Press the shutter. Then whisper: "Never let this leave me."

5. Store it somewhere safe - a hard drive, a scrapbook, a scar in your memory. A place that grief can't touch and time can't erase.

Because sometimes the camera sees the magic we're too busy or tired to notice.

Spell for Saying
Good Night Forever

Ingredients:

A photograph or item that reminds you of them
A soft piece of fabric (pillowcase, blanket, tie, scarf)
Moonlight, if you can find it
Words you never got to say

Directions:

1. Hold the item close to your chest. Let your heartbeat tell it what you can't say aloud.

2. Spread the fabric across your bed, a chair, or your lap-wherever you feel most like a child again. Somewhere quiet. Somewhere safe.

3. Speak the words you never said. Out loud or in your mind. Let them float into the night like breath on a windowpane.

4. When you're ready, say:

> "Sleep well, wherever you are.
> I'll carry your love in my waking hours,
> And meet you again in my dreams."

5. Lay your head down. Let the silence become a lullaby. Let the goodbye be soft. And let the night hold what your arms no longer can.

Spell for When the Ocean of Grief Tries to Swallow You

Ingredients:

A small palm-sized stone
Ash or paper with a loved one's name
A glass jar of stream or rainwater
A single feather or leaf
A quiet moment of breath

Directions:

1. Hold the stone. Feel its weight. Let it represent the grief-what you've carried, what you're ready to set down.

2. Drop the ash or name. Into the jar of water. Watch it drift or sink. Say their name aloud. Let it echo.

3. Add the feather or leaf. As a symbol of what returns. What carries them forward.

4. Whisper into the jar. One memory. One thank you. One goodbye.

5. Pour the water. Back into the earth-into a stream, onto the roots of a tree, or wherever life begins again.

Repeat as often as you need to. Grief takes time to process.

Don't let anyone rush your healing.

Spell for the Kind of Love That Waits

Ingredients:

Two hands willing to stay
One sacred habit, repeated with love
A scent from long ago
One returned object, marked by memory
A quiet belief in signs

Directions:

1. Say their name - the one who made ordinary feel sacred and holy.

2. Hold the object that shouldn't have found its way back to you. Let it speak to you.

3. Whisper:

> "Where you go, I will follow.
> Across war-torn maps and garden beds.
> Through morning paper and hospital sheets,
> Through lifetimes and faded red scuffs-
> I will find you again."

4. Close your eyes. Picture *their* smile.

Repeat when you need proof that love outlives breath.

"True love doesn't vanish. It waits."

Spell for the Grace of Forgiveness

Ingredients:

A small stone (to represent the hurt you've held)
A piece of paper and a pen (for what needs to be released)
A ribbon or thread (to symbolize reconnection)
A bowl of water (for gentle cleansing)
A quiet space to reflect

Directions:

1. Sit with the stone in your hand. Name what hurt you - silently or aloud. Let it rest in the weight of the stone.

2. On the paper, write what you're ready to forgive - even if it's only part of it. Be honest.

3. Forgiveness is not perfection; it's a beginning.

4. Fold the paper and wrap it gently with the ribbon. Tie it once - not to bind, but to honor your willingness to hold love again.

5. Dip the bundle briefly into the water. Let the droplets carry away resentment, and soften what has hardened in you.

Remember: it's okay to forgive someone who didn't ask for it. It's okay to forgive yourself. It's okay to forgive, but never forget.

"Forgiveness is yours to make and yours to keep."

Spell for When Time Moves Too Fast

Ingredients:

One item from your child's babyhood
A clock or watch
A quiet corner where memories still echo

Directions:

1. Place the item in front of you.

2. Hold the clock in your hands and still its ticking.

3. Close your eyes and breathe in the now -

> The giggles in the hallway.
> The fingerprints on the fridge.
> The shoes left by the door.

4. Then speak:

> "Pause the rush, if just a breath,
> Slow the hands that race toward death.
> Let this room be stitched in gold,
> A moment kept, a story to be told."

> "Though time may fly and babies grow,
> May this love be all they know.
> I was here, I saw it all –
> The rise, the fall, all the tiny calls."

5. Take one final deep breath. Whisper thank you to the air. Then let time resume - but softer now, because you remembered to notice.

Spell for Returning to Your True Self
(A sensory spell inspired by Donna)

Sight: Find one thing around you that is soft. Let your eyes land there. Stay.

Touch: Place one hand over your heart, the other on your belly. Feel the warmth of your own body holding you.

Sound: Close your eyes. Listen. Even to the quiet. Even to your own breath. Especially to your own breath.

Smell: Inhale deeply. Whether it's laundry soap, rain-soaked air, or the faint scent of your skin - take it in.

Taste: Place something sweet or soothing on your tongue-tea, honey, or nothing at all. Taste and remember: this body, your body, deserves kindness.

Speak: Whisper something nice about yourself in the universe, and believe it.

Repeat when you just don't feel like yourself anymore.

Spell for When You're Ready
to Hear the Little Voice Inside You
(Only when you're ready to listen)

Step One: Prepare the Garden
Find a quiet space, even if it's only in your mind.
Find the light. Sunlight, a lamp, anything.

Step Two: Make the Invitation
 Close your eyes and breathe slowly. Visualize
your child self entering the room or garden.
Notice how she stands. What her eyes are
telling you.

Step Three: Let Her Speak
 Let her say all the things she was never
allowed to. Don't correct her. Don't shame her.
Just *listen.*

When she's done, tell her:

> *"Everything you feel is valid.*
> *You deserved better.*
> *And you deserve love now."*

Above all else, please remember this:

You are not what happened to you.
Bad things happen to good people.

And even in the dark -
Always keep the light on.

"If trauma can be inherited, **so can love**. Be careful what you pass on. I encourage you to simply be the change you always wished for. It's inside you, it always has been. You've got this. I believe in you."

With all my love and magic,

-BARB

Resources for the Wounded, Watchful, and Healing

No matter how dark your story has been, *you are not alone.* I encourage you to self-reflect, place yourself in a positive environment surrounded by positive influences, and get into see a therapist for talk therapy.

A special thank you to Donna Lockaby, www.lockabycounseling.com.

If you are reading these pages and feel a familiar ache—if your childhood mirrored even a fraction of what's written here—I want you to know that help exists. *Healing is possible.* You are never too broken, too late, or too far gone to reclaim your light. *Never.*

If you are witnessing someone else in danger - say something. Report it. Protect the child. Be the adult you wish someone had been for you. You could save a life.

There is power in reaching out, even if your voice trembles.

Below are resources where trained professionals are ready to listen, support, and help you take the next step:

NATIONAL RESOURCES (U.S.)

Childhelp National Child Abuse Hotline
1-800-4-A-CHILD (1-800-422-4453)
childhelphotline.org
Available 24/7. Free. Confidential. For survivors and those concerned about a child's safety.

National Domestic Violence Hotline
1-800-799-SAFE (7233)
Text: START to 88788
thehotline.org

RAINN – Rape, Abuse & Incest National Network
1-800-656-HOPE (4673)
rainn.org
24/7 confidential support for sexual assault survivors.

National Suicide & Crisis Lifeline
Dial or Text: 988
988lifeline.org

IF YOU'VE WITNESSED ABUSE:

If someone is in immediate danger, call 911.

To report suspected abuse or neglect, call Child Protective Services in your state.

You can also contact Childhelp at 1-800-4-A-CHILD for guidance on how and where to report.

www.ingramcontent.com/pod-product-compliance
Lightning Source LLC
Chambersburg PA
CBHW051643120626
46551CB00015B/2193